Dedicated to the
honor and memory of
Colonel James
"Nick" Rowe, USA

(Cover) Arlington National Cemetery. (Cover inset) Eternal flame, grave of President John F. Kennedy.
(Page 1) Memorial Amphitheater. (Facing) White marble headstones.

Produced by Elliott & Clark Publishing, Washington, D.C.
Designed by Carla Frank
Edited by Carolyn M. Clark
Printed and bound in Hong Kong through Mandarin Offset
Photography c 1994 by Cameron Davidson. All rights reserved.
Text c 1994 by Owen Andrews. All rights reserved.
No part of this book may be reproduced in any manner without written permission from the
publisher except for brief quotations used in reviews.

Any inquiries should be directed to:
The Preservation Press
National Trust for Historic Preservation
1785 Massachusetts Avenue NW
Washington, DC 20036

The National Trust for Historic Preservation is the only private, nonprofit organization chartered by
Congress to encourage public participation in the preservation of sites, buildings, and objects significant
in American history and culture. In carrying out this mission, the National Trust fosters an appreciation
of the diverse character and meaning of our American cultural heritage and preserves and revitalizes the
livability of our communities by leading the nation in saving America's historic environments.

Support for the National Trust is provided by membership dues, contributions, and a
matching grant from the National Park Service, U.S. Department of the Interior, under provisions
of the National Historic Preservation Act of 1966. The opinions expressed here do not
necessarily reflect the views or policies of the Interior Department.

98 97 96 95 94   5 4 3 2 1

Library of Congress Cataloging-in-Publication Data
Andrews, Owen, 1957-
A moment of silence : Arlington National Cemetery / text by Owen Andrews ;
photography by Cameron Davidson
p. cm.
ISBN 0-89133-223-5
1. Arlington National Cemetery (Va.) — History.
2. Arlington National Cemetery (Va.) — Pictorial works. I. Title.
F234.A7A48 1994
975.5'295 — dc20   93-27115

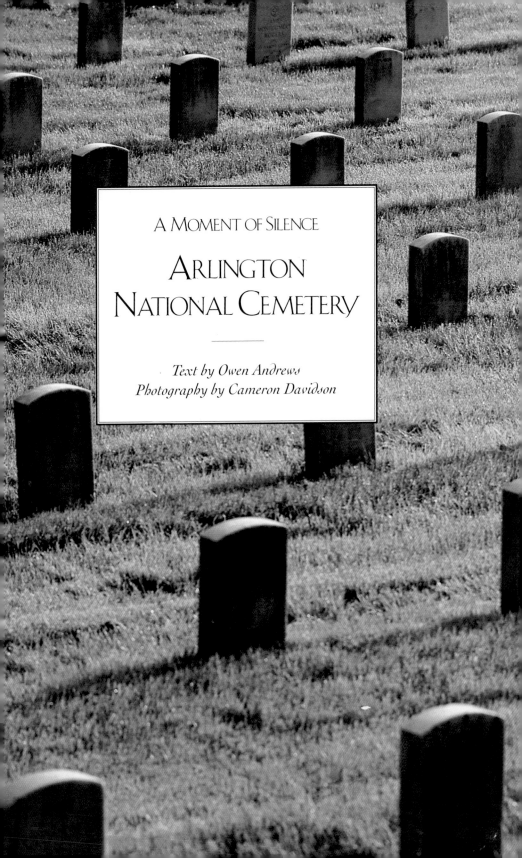

A MOMENT OF SILENCE

ARLINGTON
NATIONAL CEMETERY

Text by Owen Andrews
Photography by Cameron Davidson

No one can go there and
wander among its
monuments to the dead
and see the great names
on those monuments
without being im-
pressed, without having
his patriotism stirred,
without being brought
to a higher sense of
what the nation means
and what the people of
the nation may die for.

— Ivory Kimball of the
Grand Army of the
Republic, asking
Congress to fund
Memorial Amphitheater,
1912

ARLINGTON National Cemetery is a historic place, and yet, like any cemetery, it is not primarily a place where history happens. It is where history is remembered. Starting from the tombstones of the people buried here—the famous, the obscure, and the unknown—we can venture back into almost any corner of American history. And though the majority of the dead whose names we recognize are known for their military deeds, there are also many names made familiar through accomplishments in other fields, from Joe Louis, the heavyweight boxer, to Dashiell Hammett, the mystery writer, and from Pierre L'Enfant, the planner of Washington, D.C., to Thurgood Marshall, the Supreme Court justice.

The roster of the famous certainly contributes to Arlington's unique place among American shrines. But, as John J. Pershing, commanding general of the American Expeditionary Force in World War I, implied when he requested a simple regulation headstone for his grave at Arlington, generals are no more important than the soldiers who fight with them. Perhaps that is one reason why one of the cemetery's most revered sites is not the grave of a

Arlington is a resting place for famous Americans from all walks of life, including city planner Pierre L'Enfant, boxing champion Joe Louis, fighter pilot Gregory "Pappy" Boyington, and Supreme Court Justice Thurgood Marshall.

president or a general, but the Tomb of the Unknowns.

The Tomb, guarded 24 hours a day, 365 days a year, by an elite unit within the Third Infantry of the United States Army, is one of the three most visited sites within the cemetery's 612 acres. The other two are Arlington House, a mansion linked since its inception to great names in American history, and the grave of President John F. Kennedy, marked by an eternal flame. These three sites are more than focal points in Arlington's landscape. They mark three distinct phases in the history of the cemetery and its evolution as the principal place where the United States honors its heroes.

As a child, did he play on some street in a great American city? Did he work beside his father on a farm in America's heartland? Did he marry? Did he have children? Did he look expectantly to return to a bride? We will never know.

— Ronald Reagan; service for Vietnam Unknown, 1984

The Tomb of the Unknowns began with the burial in 1921 of an unknown American soldier from World War I.

*Arlington's South
Post area was
transferred from
Fort Myer to the
cemetery in 1966.*

WE OWE the existence of Arlington as a national military shrine in large part to the actions of three military men: George Washington, Robert E. Lee, and Montgomery Meigs. George Washington's contribution was his decision as President to site the proposed national capital on the Potomac River between the ports of Georgetown and Alexandria, a few miles upriver from his home at Mount Vernon. And it so happened that on the Virginia side of the proposed federal district lay a 1,100-acre tract belonging to Washington's wife's family.

The property, which spread from a prominent bluff to the banks of the Potomac, had been purchased in 1778 by John Parke Custis, Martha Washington's son from her first marriage. Serving as an aide-de-camp to Washington, Custis became ill during the siege at Yorktown in 1781 and died soon after, leaving his wife and four small children. The Washingtons, who had no children of their own, raised Martha's two youngest grandchildren, George Washington Parke Custis and Eleanor Parke Custis.

George Washington Parke Custis adored his foster father, and after

In the long history of the world, only a few generations have been granted the role of defending freedom in its hour of maximum danger. I do not shrink from this responsibility, I welcome it.

—John F. Kennedy, Inaugural Address; inscribed on wall near his grave

Washington's death in 1799, Custis was eager to honor his memory. When he took possession of the Custis property at Arlington in 1802, he resolved to build a mansion there that would be a shrine to the general and president. At auctions which the family held to sell Washington's personal belongings, Custis spent thousands of dollars buying as many items as possible, including clothes, camp tents from Yorktown, captured British battle flags, and the bed in which Washington died.

Taking advantage of the estate's site directly across the Potomac from the new capital, Custis built a house with a massive Doric portico perhaps inspired by the temple of Hephaestus in Athens. The result, as Robert E. Lee once said, is a "house that anyone could see with half an eye." Custis had planned to call his house Mount Washington. But Bushrod Washington, the president's nephew, objected, so Custis settled on Arlington, the name of the original Custis plantation on Virginia's eastern shore.

From its earliest days, Arlington House was a part of Washington's public landscape. Custis liked to show guests his "Washington treasury," and he also encouraged picnickers from the city to enjoy a pleasant glade with a spring near the riverbank—even building a dance pavilion there.

Custis and his wife had only one child live to adulthood, Mary Anna Randolph Custis, born in 1808. Her choice of a husband was a distant cousin and familiar face from childhood, Robert E. Lee of Alexandria, a sixth-generation Virginian and a lieutenant in the United States Army who had recently graduated second in his class at West Point.

Robert and Mary were married in the parlor at Arlington House on June 30, 1831. Over the next thirty years, Lee's military career took him to posts all over the country, but Arlington House was the family's true home. Mary Custis Lee and the children (there were eventually seven) lived there with her parents whenever it was impractical to be with Lee. Lee was often able to arrange long sojourns at the estate, which his wife held in trust for her eldest son after

The American Greek Revival style, of which Arlington House is an early and well-known example, swept the country between 1800 and 1830.

George Washington Parke Custis's death in 1857.

Lee was at Arlington House in the spring of 1861, as the country stood at the brink of civil war. He had been ordered home in February from his regiment in Texas, and on April 17, he received a summons from Washington that compelled him to make the most important decision of his life. Winfield Scott, the 75-year-old General in Chief of the United States Army, regarded Lee as the best officer in the army and hoped he could be persuaded to take command of all the Union forces. President Lincoln agreed with Scott and asked Francis Blair, a veteran of Washington politics, to relay the offer of the command.

Lee refused the Union offer. Although he opposed secession, he could not campaign against his fellow Southerners. Instead, he said, he would resign from the army and remain in Virginia, which he hoped would stay neutral. One day later, he learned that Virginia had seceded, and after withdrawing to his bedroom in Arlington House for several hours, he came downstairs after midnight with a letter of resignation from the United States Army and a letter to General Scott explaining his decision. He went to the state capital at Richmond at the request of Governor John Letcher, where, on April 22, he was offered the

The Tomb Guards at the Tomb of the Unknowns are members of the Third United States Infantry, "The Old Guard."

Duty is the
sublimest word
in our language.
Do your duty
in all things.
You cannot do
more, you should
never do less.
—Robert E. Lee

The Confederate Memorial, dedicated in 1914, honors the 409 Confederate soldiers buried at Arlington. (Facing) Dogwood is one of approximately 300 tree species at Arlington.

command of all Virginia's forces with the rank of major general, which Lee accepted.

Lee's decision drew Arlington House into the tide of war. On its bluff directly across the Potomac from the Union capital, the estate could be either a part of the city's defenses or a fine place for would-be attackers to aim artillery at the city. From

Richmond, Lee repeatedly urged his wife to pack up the family's belongings and move to a safer part of the state. In mid-May an emissary from Washington informed her that Federal troops would occupy the property, and around May 20, she finally moved, leaving many family possessions, including some of her father's Washington memorabilia, behind.

In 1861, most people believed the war would be brief. In that spirit, the Union soldiers who occupied Arlington attempted to treat the estate with respect. Gen. Irvin McDowell wrote Mrs. Lee on May 30 that "It will be my earnest endeavor to have all things so ordered that on your return you will find things as little disturbed as possible." But as the war lengthened, McDowell's "earnest endeavor," like many other chivalric niceties, was overrun by harsher interests.

Arlington House was now in the hands of the United States government, where it has remained ever since. The house quickly became a headquarters and officers' billet, and troops camped on the grounds, dug earthworks, and cut the estate's fine trees for firewood. Several forts were constructed, including Fort Whipple, the precursor to Fort Myer, just north of the cemetery; and Fort McPherson (McKinley Drive, in what is now Section 11, follows this fort's outlines).

In 1861, troops merely occupied Arlington; it still belonged to Mrs. Lee. In 1862, Congress passed a law to tax Confederate properties. The levy on Arlington was $92.07, but when one of Mrs. Lee's relatives went on her behalf to the tax office in Washington, officials there demanded that the owner pay in person. This she could not do, and the property was confiscated and auctioned to a single bidder, the federal government, for $26,800 in January 1864.

The Union had taken another step toward altering

I rode out to my dear old home but so changed it seemed but as a dream of the past — I could not have realized that it was Arlington but for the few old oaks they had spared.

—Mary Custis Lee, after a visit to Arlington House, early 1870s

The Tomb of the
Unknowns and Memorial
Amphitheater stand
where a freedman's
village once existed.

the property in June 1863, when a village for former slaves was established south of the house, beyond where the Memorial Amphitheater now stands. The Freedman's Village existed for more than 30 years, with a population, at its height, of some 2,000 people. In time, over 3,800 people from this village would be buried at Arlington (Section 27).

But 1864 was the year that altered Arlington irrevocably. The Union army needed to find somewhere near Washington to bury soldiers from the city's hospitals and from nearby battles. On June 15, Montgomery Meigs, the Quartermaster General of the Union Army, submitted

Walk softly about this place…They have gone into the tent for the night, their heads on pillows of dust, their arms stacked, their march ended, their battle fought. Sleep on, great host, till the morning light strikes through the rifts of the tents and the trumpet sounds the reveille of the Resurrection.

—Reverend De Witt Talmadge, Decoration Day service at Arlington, 1873

Union Private William Henry Christman was the first soldier buried at Arlington National Cemetery.

a written proposal to Edwin Stanton, the Secretary of War, to use the Arlington estate, and Stanton signed orders to that effect the same day.

Their agreement formalized a practice that had already begun. On May 13, William Henry Christman, a Pennsylvanian private who never saw combat and who had died of peritonitis, was buried about half a mile from the house. Christman was not the first person known to be buried at Arlington. Mary Randolph, a distant relative and friend of the Custises who died in Washington, had been buried just north of the house in 1828. The Custises themselves were also buried on

An equestrian statue, one of two in the cemetery, marks the grave of Gen. Philip Kearny, USA, killed in 1862 at the Battle of Chantilly.

the estate (now Section 13), as were some of their slaves (Section 27). Christman, however, was the first Civil War soldier to receive a military burial at Arlington.

Union officers who lived in the house had buried Christman and other casualties as far from the house as possible. But in his June 15 proposal to Stanton, Meigs wrote, "I recommend that...the land surrounding the Arlington Mansion, now understood to be the property of the United States, be appropriated as a National Military Cemetery."

Meigs, like Lee, was a Southerner, a West Pointer, and an engineer. Meigs was born in Georgia, and, not long after his graduation

Not for fame or reward, not for place or for rank, not lured by ambition, or goaded by necessity, but in simple obedience to duty as they understood it, these men suffered all, sacrificed all, dared all, and died.

— Inscribed on Confederate Memorial

from West Point in 1836, he worked with Lee on a Mississippi River engineering project. Unlike Lee, however, Meigs sided with the Union, not his native state, when the Civil War came. The war cost Meigs a son. Brevet Maj. John R. Meigs was killed on October 3, 1864, an event which probably added an element of personal bitterness to Meigs's feelings about the Confederacy.

Meigs soon ordered 65 graves dug near the house, including a few outside the fence to the Lees' rose garden. By the year's end, 7,000 Union soldiers had been interred. By 1882, 16,000 Civil War soldiers would be buried at Arlington. Those

numbers include blacks who served in the Union Army and whose graves are marked "USCT"—United States Colored Troops. They also include 409 Confederates, the first of whom was an unknown casualty interred just a few days after Private Christman.

After the war ended in 1865, the military cemetery at Arlington continued to grow. In 1866, the remains of 2,111 unknown soldiers from Bull Run and other battles were gathered in a common grave in the rose garden and covered with a huge granite sarcophagus— Arlington's first tribute to unknown soldiers and its first war memorial (Section 26). On May 30, 1868, the first memorial day, then called Decoration Day, was decreed by Gen. John A. Logan. A large crowd of people came to Arlington to hear speeches and prayers and watch war orphans decorate the graves with flowers and evergreens. In 1874, a wooden amphitheater, now called the Old Amphitheater, was completed to accommodate the crowds (Section 26), and in 1888, Congress made Memorial Day a national holiday.

In these years, the cemetery was essentially a Union shrine. The ornate graves of Union officers began to fill the ridge south of the house and the woods to the west (sections 1, 2, and 13). The heir to the property, George Custis Lee, did receive $150,000 when the United States bought the property in 1882 after the Supreme Court upheld his victory in a suit that charged the government with illegally seizing the estate. At that time, the cemetery still occupied only 200 acres of the former estate; the rest was used for other military and government purposes. In 1889, the cemetery expanded, adding 146 acres, and, in 1897, 56 acres.

Two events around the turn of the century would help turn the cemetery into a truly national site. The first was the Spanish-American

(Facing) White marble headstones were specified by the federal government for national cemeteries in 1872. (Below) Maj. Gen. Wallace Fitz Randolph requested that a cannon mark his grave.

Each year, for Memorial Day, soldiers of the Old Guard place a flag on every grave in Arlington.

A mast from the USS Maine, which blew up in the harbor at Havana, Cuba, in 1898, forms the centerpiece of the monument to the casualties of that disaster.

(Pages 28-29) Memorial Ampitheater was built between 1915 and 1920. Memorial services are held here on Memorial Day, Veterans Day, and other occasions.

War of 1898. After the USS *Maine* blew up in Havana harbor, allegedly because of Spanish sabotage, soldiers old and young, Confederate veterans among them, rushed to fight the decrepit Spanish empire. The reburial of 151 casualties from the *Maine* at Arlington in 1899 and the dedication of the Spanish-American War Memorial in 1902 brought Confederate veterans to Arlington. National pride also led to the creation of monuments to the Rough Riders (1905), to nurses who died in the war (1906), and to the USS *Maine* (1912). The center-piece of the *Maine* monument is a mast from the *Maine* itself, which was salvaged from Havana harbor and stands over the area where 229 casualties of the explosion are buried.

Meanwhile, in 1900, Congress made a move toward giving the cemetery a truly national character by voting to establish a "Confederate section" (Section 16). Confederates from other parts of the cemetery and from other cemeteries around Washington were reinterred there in 1901. In 1906, Congress approved the building of a Confederate memorial. The United Daughters of the Confederacy raised the money and chose Moses Ezekiel, a sculptor who attended the Virginia Military Institute and fought at the battle of New Market,

When we assumed the soldier, we did not lay aside the citizen.

— George Washington, letter to Continental Congress, 1775; inscribed on Memorial Amphitheater.

We here highly resolve
that these dead shall not have
died in vain.

—Abraham Lincoln, Gettysburg Address;
inscribed on Memorial Amphitheater

to create the monument. The monument was dedicated on June 4, 1914, in a ceremony at which President Woodrow Wilson spoke. Ezekiel was buried at the monument in 1921.

A s the cemetery cast off the partisan sentiments of the 19th century in the first two decades of the 20th, it also began to bear witness to the United States's deepening sense of history and its emergence as a major world power. Veterans of the Revolutionary War and the War of 1812 were moved to the cemetery from other nearby burial grounds. Thenceforth, Arlington's

Memorial Amphitheater's neoclassical design echoes the appearance of Arlington House and of Washington's federal buildings.

dead would represent every war in which the country has fought. In the same period, the Grand Army of the Republic, a Union veteran's group, was making plans for an even greater tribute to American military dead: a permanent Memorial Amphitheater with room to seat 5,000 people.

When President Woodrow Wilson laid the amphitheater's cornerstone on October 13, 1915, the United States was struggling to stay clear of a terrible world war. But by the time the Roman-style amphitheater, constructed of Vermont marble, was dedicated, over 4 million American soldiers had served with the American Expeditionary

Force in France, helping the Allies defeat the German empire in 1918. One hundred twenty-six thousand Americans had given their lives for that victory. Those numbers were small beside the 10 million deaths among the soldiers of the other Allies and the Central Powers, but staggering for a nation that had seen no major wars since 1865.

And for this war, fought with poison gas, long-range artillery, and machine guns along miles of trenches where an advance of a few yards could cost tens of thousands of lives, the old memorials—men on horseback, women in flowing robes on pedestals—seemed inadequate. So a new kind of

memorial came into existence after World War I: a tomb of an unknown soldier, chosen to represent all the unidentified dead of his country's armed forces. The idea originated in France, which buried the remains of an unknown soldier in the Arc

The Marine Honor Guard participates in a wreath ceremony at the Tomb of the Unknowns.

de Triomphe in Paris on November 11, 1920. On the same day, an English unknown soldier was buried at Westminster Abbey, and on November 4, 1921, an Italian unknown soldier was buried in front of the monument to King Victor Emmanuel in Rome.

Seven days later, on Armistice Day of 1921, the American unknown soldier arrived at Arlington in a ceremony attended by President Warren G. Harding, Gen. John J. Pershing, hundreds of dignitaries, and thousands of citizens. The unknown soldier was chosen in a process that became the pattern of the ceremonies for the unknown soldiers of World War II and Korea.

In October 1921, four American soldiers buried at cemeteries in France were disinterred. In identical coffins, their bodies were brought to the city hall in Chalons-sur-Marne. There, Sgt. Edward Younger, a veteran who had been wounded twice and received the Distinguished Service Cross, picked the unknown soldier by placing a white carnation on one coffin.

The body was shipped home on the USS *Olympia*, and on November 10, it lay in state in the Capitol Rotunda on the catafalque that had carried the remains of Abraham Lincoln. On November 11, Armistice Day, the coffin was placed on a caisson drawn by six horses

and conveyed from the Capitol to the White House and then to Arlington in a huge cortege.

A massive traffic jam on the bridge across the Potomac delayed the arrival of many dignitaries at Arlington, including President Harding, who, along with other older mourners, had left the cortege at the White House to drive the rest of the way.

In the Memorial Amphitheater, after President Harding had given a speech, he placed the Medal of Honor and the Distinguished Service Cross on the coffin. These honors, the highest an American sol-

Near the end of a military burial, the Honor Guard folds the American flag and presents it to the next of kin.

THIS MONUMENT WAS ERECTED IN 1938
AND REDEDICATED IN 1971
TO COMMEMORATE DEVOTED SERVICE
TO COUNTRY AND HUMANITY BY
ARMY, NAVY, AND AIR FORCE NURSES

dier can receive, were followed by honors from all the other Allied nations and flowers from an American and an English mother. Riflemen fired three volleys, a bugler played taps, and the ceremony ended.

With the interment of the unknown soldier, Arlington's ceremonial center shifted from the mansion surrounded by Civil War dead to the plaza of Memorial Amphitheater. New memorials appeared near the Amphitheater and the Tomb of the Unknown Soldier. The losses of World War I were honored with the Argonne Cross, dedicated to the American soldiers killed in the bitter struggle for the Argonne (Section 18); the

Canadian Cross of Sacrifice, a tribute to the U.S. troops who fought with Canadian forces before the United States entered World War I, and also to Americans who fought with Canadians in World War II and Korea (Section 46); and the Nurses Memorial, which overlooks the graves of many Army and Navy nurses (Section 21).

The period between the wars also brought changes to Arlington House, which had been used as offices and living quarters by cemetery employees since the Civil War. Congress dedicated the house in memory of Robert E. Lee in 1925, and the house was placed under the jurisdiction of the Department of the Interior

(Facing) The Nurses Memorial, dedicated in 1938, commemorates military nurses. (Above) The Canadian Cross of Sacrifice was given by Canada in 1927 to honor Americans who fought with Canadians.

in 1933. Later it was added to the National Register of Historic Places.

Goaded perhaps by the traffic jam of 1921, Congress approved the building of a bridge between the Lincoln Memorial and the cemetery. Arlington Memorial Bridge,

with its massive gilded statues, opened in 1932, and the approach to the cemetery became even more impressive when Memorial Gate was completed in 1937.

But the changes wrought upon Arlington are caused mostly by tragedies. World War II, like World War I, was a war the United States vainly hoped to keep clear of, a hope that failed completely with the Japanese attack on Pearl Harbor on December 7, 1941. When the war ended in 1945, 292,100 Americans had died in the European, African, and

Pacific theaters.

Before an unknown soldier from World War II had been selected, Americans were fighting in Korea. In May of 1958, five years after the end of that conflict, the burial of unknown soldiers from both wars took place. As in 1921, a highly decorated enlisted man made each of the final choices. Navy hospitalman William Charette, who received the Medal of Honor for bravery in Korea, chose the unknown soldier of World War II in a ceremony aboard the USS *Canberra* off the Virginia coast; Army Sgt. Ned Lyle, who was awarded the Distinguished Service Cross for bravery in Korea, chose the unknown soldier of the Korean War at a national

cemetery near Honolulu. The USS *Boston* then carried the Korean unknown to a rendezvous with the *Canberra*, and after the World War II ceremony, both unknown soldiers were transferred to the USS *Blandy* and carried up the Chesapeake Bay and the Potomac River to Washington.

After lying in state for a day in the Capitol Rotunda, the unknown soldiers were conveyed in a solemn procession on Memorial Day to Memorial Amphitheater, where President Dwight D. Eisenhower awarded them Medals of Honor. The weather was hot, and, according to the *New York Times*, 400 people collapsed

Let no neglect, no ravages of time, testify to the present or to the coming generations that we have forgotten as a people the cost of a free and undivided republic.

—Gen. John Alexander Logan, General Order #11, which gave orders for Decoration Day

Fades the night
And afar
Goeth day
Cometh night
And a star
Leadeth all
Speedeth all
To their rest.

— Words to a
version of "Taps"

(Above and facing)
The round-
the-clock vigil at
the Tomb of the
Unknowns began
in 1937.

of heat exhaustion along the crowded parade route and at the cemetery. The coffins were moved to their final resting places to the left and right of the original Tomb of the Unknown Soldier.

After World War II, the Tomb of the Unknown Soldier became the site of a new and remarkable form of tribute. Before 1925, the Tomb had no full-time guard or sentry. In November of that year, civilian guards were hired to stand watch over the Tomb. In March 1926, a military guard took over during the day. In 1937, to protect the Tomb from vandalism, the military instituted a round-the-clock watch that has continued ever since.

After 1948, when the Third United States Infantry, "The Old Guard," took over ceremonial duties at Arlington National Cemetery, the traditions of the soldiers who guard the Tomb began to acquire fame. Day and night, with a uniform and rifle that must pass a rigorous inspection, the Tomb Guard paces a 63-foot-long black mat between the Tomb and the steps of the plaza. Every movement is a deliberate, practiced part of his duty, and the pattern of the vigil is thought to be based upon the 21-gun salute, the nation's highest military honor. The Tomb

(Facing) In a burial with full military honors, mounted escorts accompany the caisson and casket to the grave site.

(Pages 43-44) A joint service color guard representing the U.S. Army, Navy, Marines, Air Force, and Coast Guard attends an armed forces full honor wreath ceremony at the Tomb of the Unknowns.

Guard marches 21 steps from one end of the mat to the other, turns to face the Tomb, stands at attention for 21 seconds, turns back the way he came, shifts his M-14 rifle to the shoulder between the Tomb and visitors, stands at attention for another 21 seconds, then marches 21 steps again. Each soldier conforms exactly to the ritual.

In the warmer months, between April 1 and September 30, the guard changes every half hour on the half hour when the cemetery is open during the day and every two hours when it is closed at night. From October 1 to March 31, the daylight "walk" is extended to an hour.

As impressive as the walk itself is the Changing of the Guard, when the relief commander inspects the uniform and equipment of the next Tomb Guard and gives the orders for the change. Like the sentinel's 21-step walk, the details of this ceremony are unique to the Tomb Guards, the sum of many refinements devised over the years.

About 30 members of the Third Infantry serve as Tomb Guards. They are divided into three reliefs, each on duty for 24 hours. Standards for selecting Tomb Guard candidates are extremely high, and successful candidates then undergo a nine-month training period. The candidate's responsibilities gradually increase: first he

learns to take care of his uniform and equipment; then he learns to correctly judge the length of 21 seconds; then he serves as a sentinel at night; and finally he begins taking shifts on the daytime watch.

At the end of nine

months, if the candidate proves himself in these tasks, he is tested on his knowledge of the guards' traditions, the cemetery's history, and other military lore in a 300-question exam. If he passes, he may wear the Tomb Guard badge. If he serves at the Tomb for another 12 months, the badge is awarded to him permanently. It is a great distinction, shared by only 400 Tomb Guards.

The ceremonial perfection to which the Tomb Guards aspire epitomizes the pride and performance of the entire Third Infantry, the First Battalion of which is stationed at Fort Myer, next to the cemetery, and Fort McNair in Washington. Since 1948, the two-fold mission of this unit, which traces its lineage to an Act of Congress on June 3, 1784, has been to protect the nation's capital and to fulfill ceremonial duties from assisting at military funerals to welcoming foreign dignitaries. Well-known units of the Third include the Continental Color Guard and the Old Guard Fife and Drum Corps, dressed in Revolutionary War uniforms, the U.S. Army Drill Team, and the Caisson Platoon, which is responsible for the caissons used in many of the military funerals at Arlington. The Third also supplies the cemetery's Army marching platoons, color guards, firing parties, and casket teams.

(Facing)
The U.S. Army band plays at a funeral with full military honors.

O N N O V E M B E R 25, 1963, a cold, sunny Monday, Washington paused once again to pay homage as a caisson drawn by six horses made its way through the streets toward Arlington Cemetery. This time, however, the cortege was for a man the nation knew well: John Fitzgerald Kennedy, the 46-year-old president, assassinated in Dallas, Texas. Following the caisson, a soldier led a riderless black horse. Empty black boots stood in the stirrups, reversed to symbolize a fallen leader.

The march to Arlington was the last step in a three-day ceremony of farewell to Kennedy in the capital. For the final cortege, mourners lined the streets from St. Matthew's Cathedral to the Lincoln Memorial, then across Memorial Bridge and up the Avenue of Heroes to Arlington's Memorial Gate. Television carried the events to an estimated 175 million viewers around the nation and millions more in 23 other countries. They watched the caisson make its way up the slope at Arlington toward the grave site, a spot just below the Custis-Lee mansion.

By the grave, after a brief ceremony, Jacqueline Kennedy lit an eternal flame. Cannons fired a 21-gun salute, a firing party shot three volleys, and a bugler

The granite stones surrounding President John F. Kennedy's grave and eternal flame were quarried in his native Massachusetts.

played taps. So ended the funeral—but not the nation's need to honor Kennedy.

In the weeks and months that followed, unprecedented crowds came to Arlington. At times, as many as 3,000 people an hour approached Kennedy's grave, and by the end of three years, 16 million had visited the temporary site with its simple, white picket fence. In 1967, the Kennedy family dedicated a permanent memorial, a terrace of rough Massachusetts granite surrounding the eternal flame and surrounded in turn by a larger stone ellipse.

Nearby, a white cross marks the grave of President Kennedy's brother, Senator and Attorney General Robert F. Kennedy. Senator

The caisson platoon at Fort Myer is now the only U.S. Army unit which keeps working horses in daily use.

Kennedy was shot and fatally wounded just after midnight on June 6, 1968, after winning the California presidential primary. Like John, Robert was a Navy veteran from World War II. Passages from the two men's speeches are carved on the walls near their graves.

The influx of visitors to the Kennedy grave required the cemetery to make changes. In quieter days, people had driven into the cemetery and parked near the area that interested them. After 1970, only relatives of those buried there would, with special passes, be allowed to drive in, and parking lots for everyone else were laid out near the cemetery's boundary. A temporary visitor's center in the 1970s and 1980s was succeeded in 1989 by a handsome permanent building on the Avenue of Heroes.

The national attention focused on Arlington by Kennedy's funeral increased requests for burials there. Another cause of the increased demand was the number of aging veterans left by two world wars and the Korean conflict. In the cemetery's first 75 years, about 50,000 people were buried there. It took less than 20 more years—from 1941 to 1959—for that number to double. A third cause was the fact that slowly, without ever quite deciding on the extent of its commitment, the United States had entered another war, this time in Vietnam. On one day at that war's height, over 40 funerals were conducted at Arlington—a tough test, even for a place that managed 23 other funerals on the day Kennedy was buried.

Although Fort Myer's 200-acre South Post was turned over to the cemetery in 1966, increasing its area to its present 612 acres, Arlington in the 1960s was rapidly running out of space. In 1967, the cemetery issued new, more restrictive eligibility requirements for inground burials. As a cemetery pamphlet explains, Armed Forces personnel who now qualify include: those who have died on active duty; those having at

Spurred boots placed backwards in the stirrups of a riderless horse signify the burial of a fallen soldier, either calvary, artillery, general, or flag rank officer.

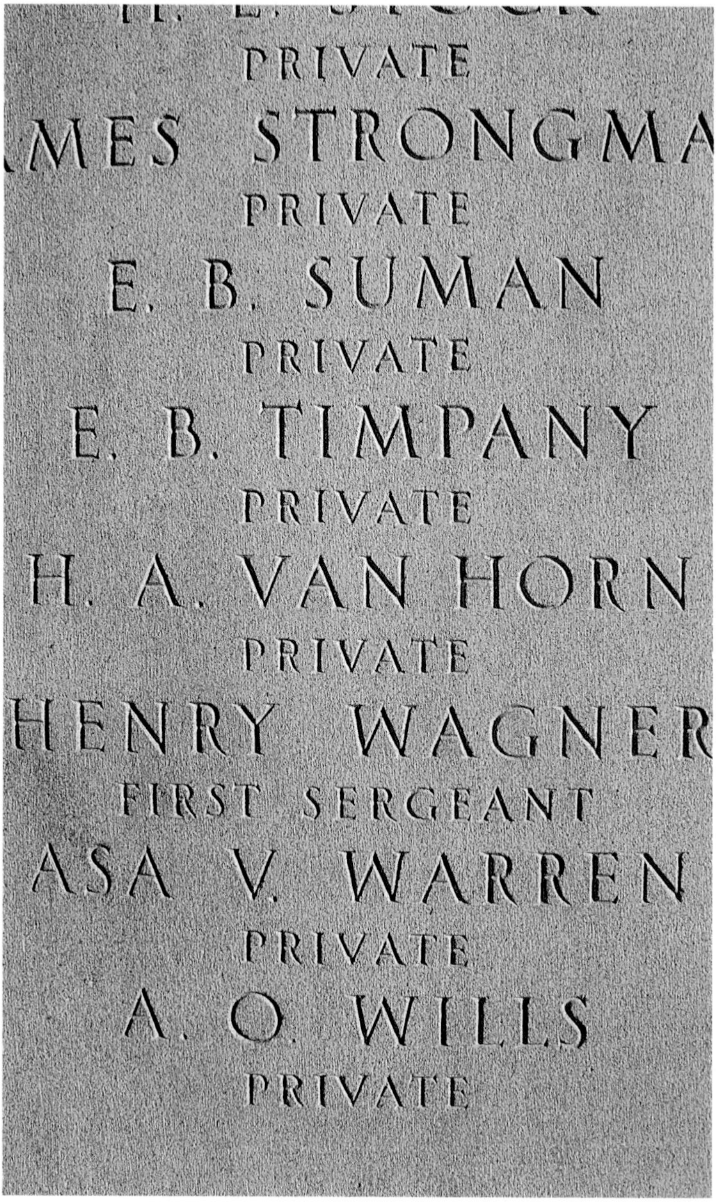

PRIVATE

MES STRONGMA

PRIVATE

E. B. SUMAN

PRIVATE

E. B. TIMPANY

PRIVATE

H. A. VAN HORN

PRIVATE

HENRY WAGNER

FIRST SERGEANT

ASA V. WARREN

PRIVATE

A. O. WILLS

PRIVATE

least 20 years' active duty or active reserve service qualifying them for retired pay; those retired for disability; holders of the Medal of Honor, Distinguished Service Cross, Air Force Cross, Navy Cross, Distinguished Service Medal, Silver Star, or Purple Heart; and veterans honorably discharged for 30% disability before October 1, 1949. In addition, spouses and dependent children of anyone in these categories and anyone already buried at Arlington qualify, as does "a veteran who is a parent, brother, sister, or child of an eligible person already interred." Eligible veterans whose remains are not recovered may be remembered with a memorial headstone. Big-band leader and U.S. Army Air Corps Maj. Alton "Glenn" Miller is one of about 2,000 veterans who have been honored in this way.

Since 1980, when the first part of a columbarium for cremated remains opened in the old South Post area, any honorably discharged veteran has been eligible for burial there. In all, the columbarium will contain 50,000 niches for urns. The cemetery, it is thought, has enough space left to continue ground burials through 2025.

The relatively peaceful years since the end of the Vietnam War have not been without some tragic losses for the Armed Forces, and these events are reflected by

(Left) A monument commemorates casualties of USS Maine *explosion.*
(Above) A cedar of Lebanon and a marker were dedicated at Arlington in 1984 in memory of 241 U.S. Marines killed in a terrorist bombing in Beirut in 1983.

We do not know one promise these men made, one pledge they gave, one word they spoke; but we do know they summoned up and perfected, by one supreme act, the highest virtues of men and citizens. For love of country they accepted death. That act resolved all doubts and make immortal their patriotism and their virtue.

— Gen. (later president) James A. Garfield, Decoration Day service at Arlington, 1868

memorials at Arlington. A monument dedicated in 1983 honors the eight servicemen who died in the 1980 attempt to rescue American hostages in Iran. A tree of Lebanon was planted in 1984 in memory of the 241 Marines killed by the terrorist bombing of the American Embassy in Beirut, Lebanon. Over two dozen of those casualties are buried near the tree. There are casualties at Arlington from the 1983 invasion of Grenada, the 1989 invasion of Panama, and the 1991 Persian Gulf War.

The largest funeral in recent years, however, was the interment, in 1984, of an unknown soldier from the Vietnam War. Congress voted to bring an unknown

soldier from that war to Arlington in 1973. But because the identification of remains had become increasingly advanced, 11 years passed before unidentifiable remains were available. The Unknown Soldier from Vietnam lay in state at the Capitol, was carried in a funeral cortege to Arlington, and was interred with full military honors on Memorial Day. President Ronald Reagan gave the address and the body was buried between the unknown soldiers of World War II and of Korea. Once again, the nation looked to Arlington to honor the memory of lives sacri-ficed in war—and the living memories of the veterans who survived.

As he changes the
direction of his
walk, the Tomb
Guard positions
his weapon away
from the Tomb of
the Unknowns.

(Pages 56-57)
Arlington now
holds over 230,000
dead and will con-
tinue to have room
for new burials
until 2025.

ACKNOWLEDGMENTS

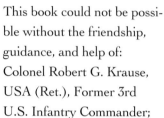

The eternal flame at the grave of President John F. Kennedy was the idea of his widow, Jacqueline.

This book could not be possible without the friendship, guidance, and help of: Colonel Robert G. Krause, USA (Ret.), Former 3rd U.S. Infantry Commander; Sgt. First Class Greg Owens, USA, Former Sgt. of the Guard; Capt. James Parker, USA; C.W. 4 Larry Duppstadt, USA (Ret.); Lt. George Davidson, USA (Ret.); Spec4 Mike Tickle, USA; Sgt. Jay Larson, USA; LTCOL. Ron Sortino, USMC (Ret.); Colonel Don Sortino, USMC (Ret.); LTCOL. Jim Vance, USMC; Capt. Chris Ellis, USMC; Sgt. Ed Sortino, USMC; W.O. 1 Mike Hedlund, USMC; Staff Sgt. Rudy Hernandez, USMC; Lt. George Eldridge, USCG, Former Officer in Charge of the USCG Honor Guard; Lt. Mark Metoyer, USCG, Former Officer in Charge of the USCG Honor Guard; Ed Rich and Caroline Despard (retired) of *Smithsonian* Magazine; Judy Connelly of *Military Lifestyle*; Susan Soroko; Carla Frank; Margaret Gore Johnson; Doug Elliott; Carolyn Clark; Doug Keefe; Tal McBride; David Rockwell and Mike Langford of Capital Color; Deputy Supt. Thurman Higginbotham, Arlington

National Cemetery; and Patty Heard of MDW Public Affairs. Thank you for your help.

        —Cameron Davidson

Several book-length works on Arlington have helped immensely in the writing of this overview. These include Peter Andrews, *In Honored Glory: The Story of Arlington;* Philip Bigler, *In Honored Glory: Arlington National Cemetery, the Final Post;* John Hinkel, *Arlington: Monument to Heroes;* James Peters, *Arlington National Cemetery: Shrine to America's Heroes;* and several sections in *Washington, D.C.: A Guide to the Nation's Capital,* originally compiled by the Federal Writers' Program and edited by Randall Truett for a 1968 reissue. *Arlington House: The Robert E. Lee Memorial,* published by the National Park Service, is also an excellent source of information.

Thanks are also due to Kathryn Shenkle, Historian's Office, Arlington National Cemetery; Robert Alley, Curator of the Old Guard Museum; and Agnes Mullins, Curator of Arlington House, for responding to questions and reviewing the manuscript. Special thanks go to Kathy for a memorable tour of the cemetery.

        —Owen Andrews

Arlington's 14,000 trees, from mature native oaks to Asian ornamentals, recall its origins as a private estate.

MONUMENTS AND VETERANS

Dates in parentheses after monuments indicate year dedicated. After names, first date indicates year of death; date after slash indicates reinterment at Arlington.

McClellan Gate, once the cemetery's main entrance, was erected in honor of Gen. George B. McClellan, USA, in the 1870s.

CIVIL WAR

Monuments

Unknown Soldiers' Sarcophagus (1866) Section 26
Old Amphitheater (1874) Section 26
Confederate Memorial (1914) Section 16
McClellan Gate (1870s—original cemetery entrance) McClellan Drive

Veterans

Pvt. William Henry Christman, USA (1864) Section 27
Gen. Philip Kearny, USA (1862/1912) Section 2

Gen. Montgomery C. Meigs, USA (1892) Section 1
Adm. David Dixon Porter, USN (1891) Section 2
Gen. William S. Rosecrans, USA (1898) Section 3
Gen. Philip H. Sheridan, USA (1888) Section 2

SPANISH-AMERICAN WAR

Monuments

Spanish-American War Memorial (1902) Section 22
Rough Riders Memorial (1905) Section 22
Spanish-American War Nurses Memorial (1906) Section 22
USS *Maine* Memorial (1912) Section 24

Veterans

Maj. Walter Reed, USA (1902) Section 3
Gen. Leonard Wood, USA (1927) Section 21

WORLD WAR I

Monuments

Argonne Cross (1923) Section 18
Canadian Cross of Sacrifice (1927) Section 46

(also honors Americans in
World War II and Korea)
United States Coast Guard
Memorial (1928) Section 4
Nurses Memorial (1938) Section 21

Veterans

Gen. John J. Pershing, USA
(1948) Section 34
Gen. Charles P. Summerall, USA
(1955) Section 30

WORLD WAR II

Monuments

USS *Serpens* Memorial (1950)
Section 34

Nearby Monuments

Seabee Memorial (1974) Memorial
Drive
United States Marine Corps
Memorial (Iwo Jima) (1954)
Netherlands Carillon (1954)

Veterans

Gen. Henry Arnold, USAF (1950)
Section 34
Gen. Omar N. Bradley, USA
(1981) Section 30
Gen. Claire Chennault, USAF
(1958)   Section 2
Sir John Dill, British Army (1945)
Section 32
James V. Forrestal, Secretary of the

Navy (1949) Section 30
Adm. William F. Halsey, USN
(1959) Section 2
Adm. William D. Leahy, USN
(1959) Section 2
Gen. George C.
Marshall,
USA (1959)
Section 7
Adm. Marc A.
Mitscher,
USN (1947)
Section 2
Gen. Jonathan
M. Wainwright,
USA (1953)
Section 1

KOREA

Monuments

Korean War
Contemplative
Bench (1987)
Section 48

Veterans

Gen. Matthew B.
Ridgway
(1993) Section 7

VIETNAM

Gen. Creighton Abrams, USA
(1974) Section 21
Gen. Daniel "Chappie" James,
USAF (1978) Section 2

*The Korean War
Contemplative
Bench, dedicated in
1987, stands near
Memorial
Amphitheater.*

The War Correspondents' Memorial, dedicated in 1987, honors journalists who have died while reporting on Americans in combat.

OTHER MEMORIALS

Tomb of the Unknowns (1921, 1958, 1984) Section 48

Memorial Amphitheater (1915-1920) Sections 48 and 35

War Correspondents' Memorial (1987) Section 46

THE SPACE PROGRAM

Monuments

Challenger Space Shuttle Memorial (1987) Section 46

Astronauts

Lt. Col. Virgil I. "Gus" Grissom, USAF (1967) Section 3

Lt. Cdr. Roger B. Chaffee, USN (1967) Section 3

Col. Francis Scobee, USAF (1986) Section 46

Capt. Michael J. Smith, USN (1986) Section 7A

Col. James B. Irwin, USAF (1991) Section 3

OTHER NOTABLES

Presidents

John F. Kennedy (1963) Section 45

William Howard Taft (1930) Section 30

Supreme Court Justices
Chief Justice William Howard Taft
  (1930) Section 30
Chief Justice Oliver Wendell
  Holmes, Jr. (1935) Section 5
Chief Justice Earl Warren (1974)
  Section 21
Justice Hugo L. Black (1971)
  Section 30
Justice Arthur Goldberg (1990)
  Section 21
Justice William O. Douglas (1980)
  Section 5
Justice Potter Stewart (1985)
  Section 5
Justice Thurgood Marshall (1993)
  Section 5

Noted Americans
Stephen Vincent Benét, poet (1943)
  Section 1
William Jennings Bryan, congress-
  man, orator, secretary of state
  (1925) Section 4
Admiral Robert Byrd, USN, polar
  explorer (1957) Section 2
Mary Custis and George Washington
  Parke Custis (1853, 1857)
  Section 13
Medgar Evers, civil rights leader
  (1963) Section 36
Dashiell Hammett, novelist (1961)
  Section 2
Matthew A. Henson, polar explorer
  (1955/1988) Section 8

Robert F. Kennedy, senator (1968)
  Section 45
Pierre Charles L'Enfant, city
  planner (1825/1909) Section 2
Joe Louis Barrow, heavyweight
  boxer (1981) Section 7A
Admiral Robert Peary, USN, polar
  explorer (1920) Section 8

*At his request, a
plain white cross
marks the grave of
Robert F. Kennedy.*

I have fought
the good fight
I have finished
my course
I have kept
the faith

—II Timothy 4:7